Have you ever felt foggy, indecisive, or emotionally stuck? What if the root of these struggles lies within your brain's biology? In Fat Brain, authors Abi Burke and Ash Burke unravel the hidden connection between excess brain fat and mental clarity. Drawing on science, practical strategies, and everyday insights, this book explores how diet, movement, and lifestyle can influence your thoughts, decisions, and emotions.

Through engaging explanations and interactive activities, Fat Brain equips you to take control of your mental well-being, rebuild your focus, and unlock the best version of yourself. It's time to nourish your brain, break free from limitations, and thrive in every area of your life.

Introduction: The Brain, Your Body's Powerhouse

When was the last time you paused and thought about your brain? Not just how it works when you're solving a problem or making a decision, but how its health might be influencing your thoughts, your feelings, and even the way you see yourself?

Most of us don't connect physical health with mental clarity. We think about what we eat in terms of our waistlines, our energy levels, or our heart health, but rarely do we stop to ask: What is this doing to my brain?

Here's the truth: the brain is deeply connected to the rest of your body. Excess fat, inflammation, and poor nutrition can clog the pathways your brain needs to work well.

When those pathways are blocked, you might notice it in subtle but life-altering ways. Decisions become harder. Relationships feel strained. You might feel lost, disconnected from your identity, or trapped in a mental fog that keeps you from living the life you want.

But the good news is this: by understanding the connection between your brain and your body, you can take back control. This book will guide you through the science in a way that's simple and practical, helping you understand how excess fat, poor habits, and inflammation might be interfering with your thoughts. More importantly, it will show you how to make changes that bring clarity, balance, and joy back into your life.

Let's dive into the journey of reconnecting with the healthiest, sharpest version of yourself.

Chapter 1: The Fat Story

Fat. It's a word that carries so much weight, no pun intended. For years, we've been told that fat is the enemy. But here's the twist: not all fat is bad. In fact, your body needs fat to survive. The key is knowing the difference between the fats that fuel your brain and the ones that fog it up.

Let's start with the good guys. Healthy fats, like omega-3s, are essential for brain function. They help build the structure of your brain and keep it flexible, which is crucial for sharp thinking and quick decision-making. These fats are like the high-quality oil you'd use in a car engine, keeping everything running smoothly.

Now, the bad guys. Excess fat, especially the kind associated with unhealthy diets and poor lifestyle choices, can cause problems. This isn't just about the fat you see around your belly or thighs. It's about what happens inside your body, including your brain.

How Fat Affects the Brain

You might be wondering: Does fat actually get into my brain? Not exactly. But here's what happens: when there's too much fat in your body, it can lead to inflammation and clogged blood vessels. Since your brain relies on a steady supply of oxygen and nutrients, anything that disrupts blood flow can impair its function.

This is where the connection to decision-making, relationships, and identity comes in. When your brain is struggling to function properly, it affects the way you think. You might feel indecisive, irritable, or disconnected. The simple act of making a choice, whether it's what to eat for dinner or how to handle a tough conversation, can feel overwhelming.

The Bigger Picture

Excess fat and poor brain health don't just stop at decision-making. They ripple out into every part of your life:

Relationships: Ever felt too exhausted or "off" to connect with someone you care about? Poor brain health can dampen your ability to empathise or communicate clearly, straining even the strongest bonds.

Identity: When your brain is foggy, it's easy to feel like you've lost touch with who you are. You might struggle to stay motivated or feel unsure about your goals and purpose.

Mood: A sluggish brain can lead to anxiety, sadness, or irritability, making it harder to enjoy life's moments.

But here's the empowering part: you can change this. By making small, intentional shifts, you can nourish your brain, reduce inflammation, and regain clarity. The rest of this book will show you how.

Next, let's dive into how excess fat affects your brain's lifeline: blood flow.

Chapter 2: Blood Flow and Brainpower

Your brain might be small compared to the rest of your body, but it's a powerhouse. Despite making up only about 2% of your body weight, it uses up to 20% of your blood supply. That's because your brain needs a constant flow of oxygen and nutrients to function.

But what happens when that flow is interrupted?

The Role of Blood Flow in Brain Health

Imagine trying to fill a glass of water when the tap is clogged. The water trickles out slowly, and it's frustratingly inefficient.

That's what happens in your brain when your blood vessels are clogged by fatty deposits or inflammation.

The brain doesn't get the oxygen and nutrients it needs to function properly, leading to sluggish thinking and impaired memory.

The Effects on Thinking and Emotions:

When blood flow to the brain is reduced, it affects the areas responsible for:

Decision-Making: Poor blood flow can weaken the prefrontal cortex, the part of your brain that helps you weigh options and make rational choices.

Emotional Regulation: The amygdala, which manages emotions, can become overactive, making you more reactive and less able to handle stress.

Memory: The hippocampus, which stores and retrieves memories, may struggle to perform, leading to forgetfulness or difficulty focusing.

These changes might show up as brain fog, difficulty concentrating, or even impulsive behavior, all signs that your brain isn't firing on all cylinders.

What You Can Do

Improving blood flow doesn't require drastic measures. Small steps, like adding more physical activity to your day and eating foods that support cardiovascular health, can make a big difference. We'll explore these in more detail later in the book.

For now, let's move on to another silent culprit that affects your brain: inflammation.

Chapter 3: Inflammation: The Hidden Saboteur

If you've ever stubbed your toe or cut your finger, you know what inflammation looks like, redness, swelling, pain. It's your body's way of protecting itself and beginning the healing process. But what happens when inflammation isn't just in your toe or finger but inside your brain?

Chronic inflammation, often caused by poor diet, lack of exercise, and excess fat, can quietly sabotage your brain. Unlike the obvious swelling you see in an injury, brain inflammation works behind the scenes, affecting how you think, feel, and even relate to others.

How Inflammation Starts in the Brain

Chronic inflammation often begins in the gut. When you eat processed foods, sugar, or unhealthy fats, your gut becomes irritated, and harmful substances can leak into your bloodstream. This triggers your immune system, creating widespread inflammation.

Once inflammation reaches the brain, it affects the delicate network of neurons responsible for processing thoughts, emotions, and memories. It's like static interfering with a radio signal, everything feels muddled.

The Impact on Decision-Making and Relationships

Inflammation in the brain can have surprising consequences:

1. Poor Decision-Making: The prefrontal cortex, your brain's rational decision-making center, is especially vulnerable to inflammation. This can make even simple choices feel overwhelming and lead to impulsive or irrational decisions.

2. Emotional Disconnect: Inflammation can reduce activity in areas like the anterior cingulate cortex, which helps you process emotions and connect

3. Struggling with Identity: When your brain is inflamed, it's harder to reflect and make sense of your experiences. This can leave you feeling lost or unsure of who you are or what you want in life.

Signs of Brain Inflammation

You might not realise your brain is inflamed, but here are some common symptoms:

Persistent brain fog or difficulty focusing.

Fatigue, even after a good night's sleep.

Mood swings or increased irritability.

Memory problems, like forgetting things you just learned.

Calming the Fire: Anti-Inflammatory Habits

The good news? You can reverse inflammation with simple lifestyle changes:

Choose anti-inflammatory foods: Opt for fruits, vegetables, nuts, and foods rich in omega-3s like walnuts or flaxseeds.

Reduce sugar and processed foods: These fuel inflammation and make your brain work harder than it should.

Stay active: Exercise helps your body release anti-inflammatory proteins, improving both your physical and mental health.

Prioritise sleep: During deep sleep, your brain clears out toxins and reduces inflammation.

Inflammation might be a hidden saboteur, but it's not unbeatable. By making these changes, you can help your brain heal and restore its clarity.

In the next chapter, we'll explore how what you eat directly fuels your brain, or holds it back.

Chapter 4: Fuel for Thought

Your brain is like a high-performance engine, it needs the right fuel to run smoothly. But unlike a car, your brain doesn't just stop working when it gets the wrong fuel; it struggles, often in ways that you might not immediately notice.

The connection between food and brain health is profound. Every bite you take has the potential to nourish your brain, or to cloud it. Understanding how the food you eat affects your thoughts, emotions, and decision-making is the next step in transforming your mental clarity and overall health.

Your Brain's Energy Needs

The brain is an energy powerhouse. Despite its small size, it uses about 20% of the calories you consume daily. But not all calories are created equal. Imagine filling your car with low-grade fuel, it might run, but not efficiently. The same goes for your brain. Processed foods, refined sugars, and trans fats may provide energy, but they leave your brain sluggish and prone to inflammation.

On the flip side, whole, nutrient-dense foods act as premium fuel, optimising your brain's function. These foods don't just energise your brain; they protect it, improve its efficiency, and even help repair damage.

Brain Fog Foods: What to Avoid

Some foods are infamous for disrupting brain health.

Here's what to watch out for:

1. Sugary Foods: Excess sugar can lead to energy spikes and crashes, impairing focus and memory. It also contributes to inflammation, which we know is harmful to the brain.

2. Trans Fats: Found in many fried and processed foods, these fats can damage the brain's cells and hinder communication between neurons.

3. Refined Carbohydrates: Foods like white bread and pastries break down quickly into sugar, giving your brain a temporary boost but leading to a sharp crash.

Brain-Boosting Foods: What to Embrace

Luckily, there are plenty of foods that fuel your brain and enhance its performance. Think of these as your mental superfoods:

Healthy Fats: Foods rich in omega-3s, like salmon, chia seeds, and walnuts, help build brain cell membranes and reduce inflammation.

Antioxidant-Rich Foods: Blueberries, spinach, and kale protect your brain from oxidative stress, which can damage cells over time.

Whole Grains: Quinoa, oats, and brown rice provide a steady supply of energy, keeping your brain sharp throughout the day.

Protein: Eggs, lean meats, and legumes are rich in amino acids, which your brain uses to produce mood-regulating neurotransmitters.

The Gut-Brain Connection

What you eat doesn't just affect your brain directly; it also impacts your gut, which plays a surprisingly large role in brain health. Your gut is home to trillions of bacteria that influence everything from mood to memory. An unhealthy diet can disrupt this balance, leading to brain fog, anxiety, and even depression.

Focus on foods that promote a healthy gut, like fermented foods (yogurt, kimchi, sauerkraut) and fiber-rich vegetables. When your gut is happy, your brain will thank you.

Practical Tips for Brain-Friendly Eating

Start small: Add one brain-boosting food to your meals each day.

Cook more at home: This helps you control ingredients and avoid hidden sugars or unhealthy fats.

Hydrate: Your brain is about 75% water, so staying hydrated is crucial for focus and clarity.

Eat regularly: Skipping meals can lead to energy dips and poor decision-making.

Fueling your brain isn't about perfection; it's about making consistent, intentional choices. When you start treating food as brain fuel, you'll notice the difference, in your thoughts, emotions, and overall well-being.

Next, we'll explore how movement and physical activity directly influence brain health and mental clarity.

Chapter 5: Move Your Body, Heal Your Mind

Think of your body as the delivery system for your brain. If your body isn't moving, your brain isn't getting the oxygen, nutrients, and energy it needs to function at its best. Exercise is often praised for its physical benefits, but its impact on the brain is just as profound, and it's something we often overlook.

The Brain-Boosting Power of Exercise

When you move your body, several things happen:

1. Increased Blood Flow: Physical activity improves circulation, ensuring your brain gets a steady supply of oxygen and nutrients. This is critical for focus, memory, and decision-making.

2. Neurogenesis: Exercise encourages the growth of new brain cells, particularly in the hippocampus, which is essential for learning and memory.

3. Stress Reduction: Movement helps lower levels of cortisol, the stress hormone, while boosting endorphins, which improve mood and reduce anxiety.

What Happens When You Don't Move?

A sedentary lifestyle can be disastrous for brain health. Lack of movement slows blood flow, leading to a buildup of toxins in the brain. Over time, this can contribute to cognitive decline, poor memory, and increased risk of conditions like Alzheimer's.

In addition, being inactive often leads to weight gain and excess fat, which, as we've seen, can trigger inflammation and impair brain function.

How to Incorporate Movement into Your Day

You don't need to run marathons or spend hours at the gym to reap the brain-boosting benefits of exercise. Here are some practical tips:

Start small: A 10-minute walk can make a big difference in your mood and clarity.

Find what you enjoy: Dancing, swimming, yoga, any movement that feels good to you will benefit your brain.

Be consistent: Aim for at least 30 minutes of moderate activity most days of the week.

Don't forget strength training: Building muscle improves metabolism and supports overall brain health.

Movement isn't just about looking good, it's about thinking and feeling your best.

Chapter 6: Sleep: The Brain's Reset Button

We live in a culture that glorifies being busy, often at the expense of sleep. But your brain doesn't get that memo. Sleep is non-negotiable for brain health. It's during sleep that your brain clears out toxins, consolidates memories, and recharges for the day ahead.

Why Sleep Matters

Lack of sleep affects your brain in profound ways:

1. Memory: Without enough sleep, it's harder for your brain to store and recall information.

2. Focus and Decision-Making: Sleep deprivation slows down your thought processes, making it harder to concentrate and make sound decisions.

3. Emotional Health: Sleep helps regulate mood. When you're sleep-deprived, you're more likely to feel irritable or overwhelmed.

Sleep and Fat in the Brain

Excess fat can interfere with sleep quality. For instance, carrying extra weight can contribute to conditions like sleep apnea, which disrupts breathing during sleep. Poor sleep, in turn, exacerbates

inflammation and impairs brain function, creating a vicious cycle.

How to Improve Your Sleep

Stick to a schedule: Go to bed and wake up at the same time every day.

Create a bedtime routine: Wind down with relaxing activities like reading or meditation.

Limit screen time: Blue light from screens interferes with your body's natural sleep signals.

Optimise your environment: Keep your bedroom dark, quiet, and cool.

Prioritising sleep is one of the most powerful things you can do for your brain.

Chapter 7: Mind Your Mindset

Your thoughts and beliefs shape your brain. If you're constantly stressed, anxious, or self-critical, your brain will reflect that. But the reverse is also true: a positive, growth-oriented mindset can literally rewire your brain for better health and happiness.

The Power of Mindset

Your brain is incredibly adaptable, thanks to a phenomenon called neuroplasticity. This means that the way you think can physically change your brain. For example, practicing gratitude or mindfulness can strengthen neural pathways associated with positive emotions and reduce stress.

How Excess Fat Affects Mindset

Excess fat in the body often leads to inflammation, which can interfere with the brain's ability to regulate mood.

This can make you feel stuck in negative thought patterns, which can impact relationships, decision-making, and your overall sense of self.

Practical Tips for a Healthier Mindset

Practice mindfulness: Spend a few minutes each day focusing on your breath or simply observing your thoughts.

Challenge negative beliefs: Replace self-critical thoughts with empowering ones.

Celebrate small wins: Recognise and appreciate your progress, no matter how small.

Your brain is listening to your thoughts, so speak kindly to yourself.

Conclusion: A New Chapter for Your Brain

Your brain is your most valuable asset. It shapes how you think, feel, and experience the world. By understanding the impact of excess fat, inflammation, and lifestyle choices, you've taken the first step toward reclaiming your mental clarity and emotional balance.

The journey isn't about perfection; it's about progress. Small, consistent changes, eating nourishing foods, moving your body, getting quality sleep, and cultivating a positive mindset, can transform your brain and your life.

You have the power to write a new story for your brain, one that's clear, vibrant, and full of possibility. Are you ready to begin?

Interactive Pages: Your Daily Brain-Health Routine

How to Use This Section

This section is designed to help you incorporate the principles of brain health into your daily routine. Each day, take 10–15 minutes to complete these steps. Consistency is key!

Step-by-Step Daily Prompts

Step 1: Morning Mind Check (5 minutes)

1. Sit in a quiet space with a notebook or these pages.

2. Ask yourself:

How do I feel this morning? (Energised, groggy, neutral?)

Did I sleep well? Write a quick note about the quality of your rest.

Is my brain foggy or clear?

3. Write one intention for the day to support your brain:

Example: "I will drink more water to stay focused."

Step 2: Movement Tracker (5 minutes)

1. Write down one physical activity you plan to do today.

Example: "Take a 15-minute walk after lunch."

2. After completing it, reflect:

Did the activity improve my mood or focus?

How can I make this movement a consistent habit?

Step 3: Nutrition and Hydration Check (5 minutes)

1. List the meals and snacks you plan to eat today.
Example: "Breakfast: Avocado on toast; Lunch: Chicken salad…"

2. Circle brain-healthy foods you've included (e.g., leafy greens, nuts, seeds, berries).

3. Set a goal to drink at least 8 glasses of water. At the end of the day, write:

"Did I meet my hydration goal? Yes/No."

"What food or drink helped me feel focused or energised?"

Step 4: Emotional Awareness (5 minutes)

1. Reflect on your emotions during the day. Ask yourself:

Was there a moment I felt stressed, overwhelmed, or calm?

How did my mental clarity affect my interactions with others?

2. Write one gratitude statement related to your day.

Example: "I am grateful for my walk in the sunshine."

Step 5: Decision Reflection (5 minutes)

1. Think of one decision you made today, big or small.

Example: "I chose to take a break from work instead of pushing through."

2. Reflect:

Was my decision clear or influenced by brain fog?

How can I support better decisions tomorrow?

Weekly Brain Check-In (Sundays)

1. Write about how your brain feels overall after following these daily steps for a week.

2. Answer the following:

What worked well this week?

What habits do I want to improve or continue?

3. Set three goals for the next week to keep your brain healthy.